Breaking the Glass

Breaking the Glass

poems by

LouAnn Shepard Muhm

Loonfeather Press
Bemidji, Minnesota

Cover design: Mary Lou Marchand
Cover and author photographs: Steven R. Peterson

First printing 2008
Printed in the United States of America
ISBN 978-0926147-26-3

This project is made possible, in part, by a grant from the Region 2 Arts Council through funding by the Minnesota State Legislature.

The writing of some of these poems was made possible in part by a grant from the Minnesota State Arts Board, through an appropriation by the Minnesota Legislature and funding from the National Endowment for the Arts.

Loonfeather Press is a not-for-profit small press organized under section 501 (c) (3) of the United States Internal Revenue Code.

Loonfeather Press
P.O. Box 1212
Bemidji, MN 56619

for Daniel and Leah

Acknowledgments

The following poems have previously appeared as listed (sometimes in a slightly different form):

"Waitress"—*Lake Country Journal, CALYX, Letters to the World* (Red Hen Press)
"The Turning"—*Dust & Fire*
"Monologue"—*Dust & Fire*
"Snapshot of My Children"—*Dust & Fire*
"Cyclic"—*North Coast Review*
"Offering"—*North Coast Review*
"Unfinished"—*Red River Review*
"Tassajara, 59 Degrees"—*Red River Review*
"Respite"—*The Talking Stick, Creekwalker*
"Nomenclature"—*Eclectica*
"The Lady of Shalott"—*Poems Niederngasse*
"Dropping the Veil"—*Alba, Creekwalker*
"Turbine"—*Alba, Creekwalker*
"Shoveling Out"—*Creekwalker*
"Pavlovian"—*Creekwalker*
"Release"—*Uncontained: Writers and Photographers in the Garden and the Margins* (Baksun Books)

My great thanks go out to all who helped in the creation and editing of the poems in this collection: my teachers CarolAnn Russell-Schlemper and Jane Hirshfield; Steve Peterson; Tiffany Besonen; Lynn Levin; Matthew Merritt; Mark Hartung; Betty Rossi, Gail Rixen and Mary Lou Marchand at Loonfeather Press; the leaders and participants of the Colrain Manuscript Conference; the members of <Northography.com> (Britt Fleming in particular); Jackpine Writers' Bloc and The Bards; Region 2 Arts Council; Minnesota State Arts Board; my dear friends; and, most importantly, my family.

Contents

Breaking the Glass

Snapshots

Turning

Afterimage

Cyclic

Archetypal

Breaking the Glass

Offering

*"I shy away
from transcendence."*
                    Bill Borden

We all do,
are all deer
in the ditch,
white tails arcing
graceful as we flee
the passing numen,
leaping away
from bright lights
and broad wheels.

Or maybe we stay quiet,
heads down,
grazing,
ignoring that flash
that has passed us by
before.

Some will stand frozen,
make a wrong step,
then, nicked and limping,
bleed into the woods.

But sometimes there is one
who runs headlong
to the road,
sacrificing everything
to get behind
that glass.

Conspicuous Consumption

Take this mess from my plate.
Give me sterile food
That doesn't bleed,
A curling strip of carrot,
A lifeless bit of bread,
Cabbage,
An onion—
Anything that isn't red.
I know plants' respiration
Is an index of a life,
But oats don't cry out when you cut them,
Peas don't scream
under the knife.

Monologue

Say it hadn't gone
like this.
Say we hadn't been
good children,
steeped dark and long
in denial's hot bath,
then polished and rubbed
to a high, hard sheen.
Say, instead, we were soft,
and allowed to say yes.
Say we were
gardeners,
spent long days
with the earth's sweet turning,
used dried blood
and ground bone
to encourage the bloom.
Say we could be
somewhere else,
not on this arid plain
with dust in our teeth
and only mirages
to walk toward.

Just say it.

Homonymic

Dance of two,
of to,
distant
and much
and love—
that, too.
Pairing,
paring,
cutting through bitter rind
deep into the flesh
of want.
Having
halving—
the part that goes on
and the part
that waits.
This desire keeps shifting—
forty-five, ninety,
a hundred eighty degrees,
until I have to see it written
to know
what it means.

Kindling

I knew I would break you,
but I wanted to do it cleanly—
over my knee
with a sharp, satisfying crack
and two equal pieces
to stack neatly
on the workbench.
The path is strewn
with splinters.

Dear Immovable Object

It's me, the Irresistible Force, although
I will have to find a new name,
having lost this battle of logic
and not-logic.
After all, there is no way
we can both exist
and be successful in our tasks,
and the Tao goes both ways;
a small rock holds back a great wave
and yet
water overcomes the stone.
I don't know if I have that kind of time,
if when I *do not-doing* it counts,
since in my head I am doing, doing, doing,
no matter how still I keep.
If no action is taken, harmony remains,
but the cacophony in my heart is
always off by one note,
and no matter how long I listen,
the dissonance demands fixing.
I resist, because
those who wish to change the world
according to their desire
cannot succeed,
and I want to succeed,
which I guess is the problem.
So, how to reconcile
the motion of the Way is to return
and
the use of the Way is to accept,
when the thing I cannot accept
is your refusal to return?

Great truth seems contradictory,
I guess is my answer.
That, and
great love incurs great expense.
I will try to remember
the follower of the Way forgets
as much as he can every day,
or am I supposed to forget that, too?
Anyway, I admire the way you can
practice no-action,
and I imagine that you
accept the world
in a way I cannot yet,
though I will keep trying.
Meanwhile,
love acts, but without reason
and
closely held beliefs are not easily released.

Breaking the Glass

I came late to truth,
afraid that the world might shatter
under its weight.

It did
and I am
so grateful.

Manifesto

I'm vain about my teeth,
but not so vain
that fear of the pit
will keep me from eating life
when I am hungry for it.

Turbine

The invisible moves
through outstretched arms
spinning power
we harness and spend
forgetting
we were made
for flight.

Transom

We listen from outside
to the scrapes and whispers
of what we cannot know,
jigsaw the pieces into a shape
that comforts or afflicts
and believe that we believe,
although this window
is not meant
to reveal anything
but light.

Refusal

The crack had been there
for weeks, just a hairline,
vertical,
never creeping more
than an inch below the rim.
I thought to throw
the glass away,
but kept it,
careful to drink from the side
that was whole.
Today, I put my hand
inside the the glass and,
as the blood bloomed
into the soapy water,
learned again
what happens.

Snapshots

Snapshot of My Children, Climbing Trees

Looking at you
perched in the branches
of a fallen tree,
I am reminded
of that wary time
when I thought
I was the only one
who knew.

Your father didn't know.

He vaguely felt
me slipping sideways
out of his tightening grasp
and reacted
to subtle, silent
currents of shift.

My rebellion wasn't open
yet
and I kept it
in the parts of my life
that you didn't occupy
thinking that there were
parts of my life
that you didn't occupy.

But it is there,
in the smile
that misses your eyes,
in the chin jutting
onto your clenched fist,
braced for the blow
you knew was coming.

Those branches are a fortress
and I dream
that while my arms are pinned
under my own weight
you find something
to hold you
up.

Nomenclature

My mother's name is Hester,
as was her mother's,
and her mother's mother's.

I asked her once
why she didn't carry
the tradition through
and she answered,
I wouldn't do that to you.

I was grateful.
Surely, I would have been teased,
as she was,
though not for the same reasons.

I mean,
nobody really reads
anymore.

But here I am
in the back of this pickup truck with you
fulfilling my destiny
anyway.

Presence

This ring, once my mother's
has become invisible to me.
Worn every moment
for twenty-five years,
donned at thirteen,
removed only to change
to a thinner finger.
Shaped like an eye—
rose-gold lid.
garnet iris—
it has seen everything I have,
and haven't.

Grist

I have kept her late again,
this eight-year-old,
winnowing her
for whatever grains
I can use
because I know
that no matter how
often I have
probed this child of chaff,
there will always be a kernel
of pain
to pick up and turn over
in my hand
dreaming of the
grand confections
I can make
with such fine-textured flour.

I am done with her
for now.

She is sitting on the curb
in front of the mill
and I wonder
what keeps her
from blowing away.

Assembly Line

Pain gets monotonous
like any other job.
I wait for a break,
fifteen minutes to be normal,
someone to relieve me
or believe me or retrieve me
but words
keep coming
down this conveyor
and I have no choice
but to inspect them
for my defects.

Respite

Loading the car for camping,
my stomach hollow
with joy and apprehension,
I knew
that if only I endured
for a few more hours
your crocodile rage
at our late departure,
the quantity of our equipment,
the age and condition of our car,
the weather, slow drivers, lost tent poles
and the general state of our being,
eventually
the constant hum of your anger
would be drowned out
by the crickets
and the wind
and for that one moment
you would be part of the circle,
not the fire
at its center.

Matriarchy

(a response to e.e. cummings)

I never wanted to come from them,
Those Cambridge Ladies.
If my soul were to be furnished, I thought,
Let it be with the stain-resistant Herculon,
Fingerprinted Formica,
And unbridled emotion
Of my more-recently-American friends;

Not with the crocheted lace antimacassars,
Spindly-legged chairs
And high-waisted taciturnity
Of those sanitized revolutionaries
And their daughters.

If anything were to be bandied about, I thought,
Let it be rage,
Or passion,
Or transcendent love;
Not those silly professors
Or the syntax of things.

If I were to be their daughter,
I would separate myself from them
With shapeliness and scent,
Believe only in the living
And never ask for blessings, Protestant or otherwise.

I would be sure that my mind was uncomfortable,
My face ever-changing
And never learn to knit.

23

What I have learned, however,
Is not how far they are from me,
But how close I want to come
To these women
And the angry fragment
Of that sugar moon.

At the Baths

Twelve-year-old girls
fall into two camps:
those so thrilled
with their budding womanhood
and burgeoning power
that they can hardly find
clothing revealing enough,
or enough eyeliner,
or surreptitious ways
to make their nipples hard
and visible,
who search for and use
the most inventive language to embody
their combined fascination and disgust
at their mother's nakedness,
or their grandmother's,
or their own,
and those,
like you,
who hunch their shoulders forward
under huge t-shirts
and peek out from behind
slightly parted curtains of hair,
who cannot walk comfortably
through a drugstore,
surrounded by all those reminders
of the body
and its functions.

Your body,
for which you have no language,
is flowering in spite of you,
ripening against your best efforts
to contain it,
and I want to bring all of you
here, to the baths,
where the hushed reverence
with which we carry ourselves
is partly for the place
and its effect,
but mostly for our own
deep-breasted
beauty.

Chameleon Face

Invariably, I remind people
of someone else they know:
my sister,
a friend of my daughter,
my cousin's teacher,
a woman I once sat next to on a plane,
and I make jokes
about my generic face
which bears so little resemblance
to my own family,
and hope that all of these people
are really in me,
as yet
undiscovered.

Turning

Talisman

This twenty-year-old,
the cousin of a friend,
has come for my old kitchen table.
She is so brilliantly young
and breathless,
in a hurry to carry
what has grown too small for me
out my door
and into her dewy new life,
and I want to stop her,
to show her the cigarette burn
in one corner,
to tell her
how we sat one morning
in bathrobes,
drinking coffee,
basking,
how you looked
as you pulled my feet
into your lap
and rubbed them with both hands,
holding your cigarette between your lips,
squinting as the smoke wafted up,
jutting your chin forward
to try to stop the ember
from falling,
how, for years,
every time I sat at the table
I touched the burn,
always aware of its presence
even under the cloth

and how strange it felt
to realize
I didn't touch it
anymore,
how this table
is the last thing left
that bears any mark of you.

The only proof I have.

Waitress

They speak to you
in Spanish
to be funny
or in response to
your dark hair and eyes
and you answer in French
so they know
this is no ordinary
restaurant,
but you laugh along
because they *are* funny
on vacation with their compadres
and they love the food
the drink
and you who bring it to them
and remember from last summer
a lime not a lemon
in their iced tea
or no salt on the margarita,
and for every one who asks
for your number
or comments on your dress
there are two who ask
what you are reading
or whether you have published
lately,
and you are there with *your* compadres
dancing out an incredible ballet
of hot plates and crushed ice
until you go home
where your husband says
you smell like quesadillas

and he likes it
and your children
to whom checks mean nothing
squeal
as you empty your pockets
of all the gleaming coins
that they can count.

The Giant Man With the Giant Hands

His eyes go cloudy describing
You know, that motion, when a woman
is walking, and she reaches up,
so casually

Here, his own hands rise
and she smooths her hair
catches it in both hands,
twists it up . . .
All one movement, so lovely

His hands and his jaw drop,
he is with her on the street,
newly anointed by the gesture
benediction, supplication,
the white undersides of her uplifted arms.

What I could do
with a man like that!

The Turning

In the small-town cafe
eating dinner with my children,
hurrying to get to the movie
in time,
I noticed his watch.
It was large
and pointed toward me
at just the right angle
for me to see
how much time
we had left.
Though it was near seven,
the watch read three-thirty
so I looked at him,
a man alone in a cafe,
eating toast with grape jelly
and only that
for dinner.

He was 70 or so,
thin and unkempt,
his wedding ring hanging loosely
and his neck lined
with bloody shaving nicks.
Something about
the movement of his jaw
as he meticulously chewed the toast
took me back to those
nursing home visits when,
overcome by the smells
of cabbage and disinfectant,

I would rush down
the gauntlet of the hall
past those wraiths in wheelchairs
who would paw at me
and call me by their daughters' names,
ask why I never visited,
cry for me to tell them
when their dead loved ones
would be there.

I wanted so badly
to throw myself at him,
a stranger in a cafe,
and cry into his shoulder

Oh, Daddy.

Unfinished

Focused on a book
of poems, front-porch swinging, the woman
cups her hand against her brow to shade her eyes.
It is not enough that there is a tree
hanging over her and no traces
of sun for her to block.

She is the only one on this well-scrubbed block
who reads, and her book
is held flat so no one traces
the oddities that build around her, a woman
who would read frivolous words beneath an elm tree
under midday eyes.

There is something in her eyes
they cannot forgive; she can block
their unsubtle attempts to tree
her like a hunted raccoon, even without her book,
and they cluck their tongues and call her "that woman"
because she is not a horse broken to the traces.

Eventually, alone in the refuge of the strange, she traces
branch fingers falling dark across the page and eyes
the prison door, waiting for a crack big enough for a woman
and her mind. She will prop it open with a block
for her sisters to follow and, like her, book
themselves passage out from under the porch tree.

Maybe it will be the tree
that she will climb to heaven, no traces
of her life in the courthouse book
to be found by descended eyes
hungry to fill in the block
on a geneological chart labeled "woman."

Until the door opens or the woman
finds her feet to climb the tree,
she will sit reading, the only one on this starched and ironed block
to pass her afternoons on the porch, the only traces
that she feels them watching in the shielded eyes,
the hand curving against the brow,
a tunnel from eye to book.

Femme Fatale

Male attention makes her wince now
And she wonders what they see,
But she knows, too,
And it scares her
To be thought of in that way.
So she argues with her suitors
And when complimented, frowns.
She knows she likes it too much.
If she lets it in,
She'll drown.

Afterimage

Echolalia

We learned our bodies' language,
complex and lovely
with its own irregularities, and,
as it turned out,
far too many subjunctives.

My knowledge of its delicate grammar fades,
but some mornings I come up out of dreams
with words on my lips
I thought I had forgotten.

My native tongue.

Afterimage

As children we were warned
not to look
but we watched on paper,
one sheet held above the other
as the shadow
sickled itself
across the pinholed light.
I peeked
when I could,
furtive and afraid,
until the burning stayed too long
and the warnings rang true
and terrible.

It is the way I look at you now,
mainly on paper,
with only the briefest
stolen glances
so as not to be blinded
by brightness
eclipsing slowly
into dark.

Pavlovian

The bowl remains empty
but your voice rings
just the same.

Hard Science

Chemistry: the only class
we ever took together.

In it we learned about bonding,
covalent,
ionic,
and the importance
of the shared
electron.

It was a conversation we continued
for twenty years
though we used different terms,
and when the test came
we failed,
having focused all of our attention
on chemistry,
and none on physics
or its inexorable laws.

Breadcrumbs

Everywhere I go
I leave a trail:
notes scribbled on a napkin in a bar,
an arrangement of leaves in the road.

I want you to be looking.
I want to be found.

You never come.

I blame the birds.

To the Beginning of the End of Self-Hatred

You arrived quietly,
sometime in my thirties,
announcing yourself by absence—
(makeup, uncomfortable shoes)
and by presence—
(unflattering hats, moments of real rest).

I walked into the driveway,
broad daylight,
in a ratty nightgown,
chatted with the neighbor,
and felt your breath.

You've become my scarecrow,
a warning
to the men who stripped me clean;
my lighthouse,
a reminder not to fling myself
onto the rocks again.

You disappear sometimes,
leaving me alone in a fitting room,
trying on bathing suits,
but your abandonments grow shorter,
or perhaps longer but I don't notice.

I release you,
with a slight shove
toward my daughter.

Love

You don't go into it
hoping for calm,
for days that go liquid
in the flow of their routine,
until you have had enough brilliant failures
to have learned
that your grandmother's silver,
worn smooth with long use,
will neither dazzle you
nor ever slip
from your hand.

Taming

Distracted by your beauty and
the slyness
of your smile, I don't
see you tossing
stones into the river's
swollen course.

You wait,
watching slant-eyed, for the waters
to recede, while I worry
about drowning
and erosion of the banks.
The water finds calm,
my reflection
claims the surface, and the glinting
rays of sunlight keep me
blinded to the depths.

Still you wait,
breathing steady,
For the clarity of twilight, while
I curse illumination and
the endlessness of day.

The light around
us softens,
the riverbed looms up
and I see
the scattered pebbles
that you wanted me to find.

They are rounded and worn smooth.
How long did you hold them?

They lost their
jagged edges
in the currents of
your heart.

Consumed

All my life
I've sliced, minced, carved,
Endlessly dividing and dividing again.

Still, those who tried
found me more than they could swallow
and spat me discreetly into napkins
when the hostess wasn't looking
or guttered and choked
until they could rid themselves
of the blockage.

Then you took me whole
and I didn't stick in your throat
but melted on your tongue
like sugar.

Whitewater

You shoot the rapids
while I wait in the calm
where the steady slap
of wave and oarstroke
whisper

Your heart.

My pulse.

Our breath.

This love.

The Fall

leaving the cliff edge behind
our pulse slows
to the beat of the rushing air
we don't think about
landing because we are flying
our stomachs dropping
away into the world
we have left so
we need not serve
anything anymore
not gravity
nor each other
but only the refrain
of our untethered breath

Too Much to Ask

You in a pith helmet
plunging into my pathless flesh,
to slog undaunted
through curtains
of knotted veins,
up to your knees
in a swamp of blood
and grease,
never turning back
until you have reached
the unrippling
river
mouth.

You are gone

not for long,
but still gone,
out of my reach,
and it is snowing,
so I drink this tea
to bring back last summer
when we spent all day
picking flowers, laughing,
running from bees,
pressing daisies, clover, violets—

One day
we found bee balm
and I told you that
Earl Grey tea tasted
the same way
that it smelled
and you said
huh.
since you never drink tea
but I know
even where you are now,
where maybe it is snowing, too,
you still hold the taste
of that day
in your mouth.

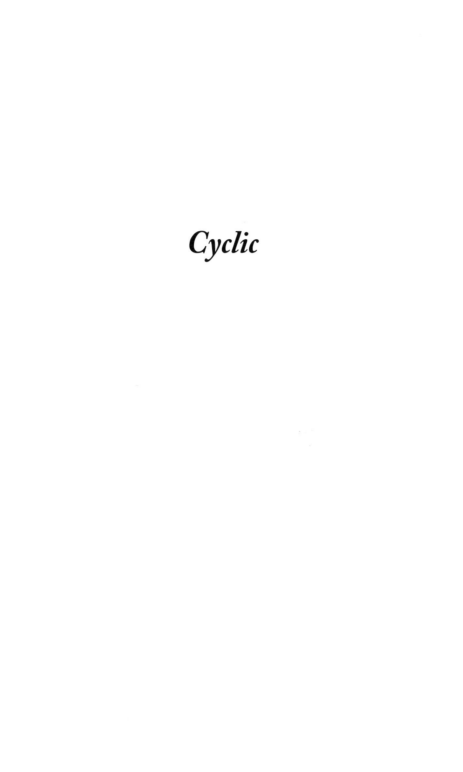

Cyclic

Inspiration

I cannot will it
to come or go,
but I can breathe
and stay alert
for that single molecule of scent,
the way the blue heron
listens.

Sage

The eagle flew
with me as I drove,
low enough to show
its tail's yellowing edge.
As I touched the brake
to prolong the moment
it curved away,
like anything
grasped.

You Wonder How It Feels to Me

Notice
how the water
parts for you,
then closes over your dive,
rings rippling
outward,
outward,
outward.

Then float,
and think
how the water must feel
to hold you there,
so still
and weightless.

Bird Sanctuary

I don't know how
word gets out—
whether in song
or in movement
like the bees' waggle-dance,
showing the way
to all the best nectar—
but somehow they know
I've learned from girlhood
to keep the feeders filled,
to open my doors
to the broken-winged
and lost.

I have no field guide
to tell by their markings
whether they are vultures,
or eagles,
or wrens,
but I take my own notes
and add more data
with each new check
on my lifetime
list.

Eating Salmon

Perfectly done,
the flesh falls
into pink feathers
against my fork
and I think of
the fight,
the salmon
tangled in the net,
and wonder
what makes futility
so delicious.

I Am Smoke When I Can Be

More often, I am water
in the shape of my container
appearing stagnant
but escaping
one molecule at a time
only to condense
and fall again
into the next low place
waiting to receive me.

Release

Days of work long past,
these flowers have outgrown
my careful tending.
No grass or weed invades
this mat of bloom,
and water gives itself
to roots grown deep.

Every night I spread bedsheets,
bundling plants
against frost,
and every morning I am proud
of having cheated death
again.

Tonight I forego
white drifts of percale,
opening the beds
to their own
final beauty.

Acorn

It always happens:
just when I think I've found a path,
built some momentum,
something appears
in the middle of it
to distract me.
Today,
an acorn,
longer and more pointed
than the ones I know.

I stop
and pick it up,
turn it over in my hand,
wonder how it will grow
into a tree
and how I will travel
down
the trunk of my life,
leaving these lofty branches,
burrowing into the dirt,
trying to see back
to that first splitting-open,

trying to see
if it looks anything
like this one.

Dropping the Veil

In winter woods
trees settle in
to their true shapes,
and the distant lake
becomes visible.

Cyclic

The imperceptible gathering
of oceans rising,
lakes surrendering themselves,
the steam of the cookpot
and my own labored breathing
has come to this
hard rain.

Shoveling Out

You've stayed away from the windows
unwilling to look at the yard
full of unfinished chores
and death
and then, overnight,
the snow,
a foot or more
a gift,
a day
maybe two if you're lucky,
of clean white forgetting
until the mailman leaves you a note,
a reminder
that beauty is treacherous.

It is not until
you get out in it
and dig
pain singing
in every muscle
that you realize
the terrible weight.

Identity

Raindrop,
as you slide down the misty pane
are you rushing to the moment of collision?

Do you stretch yourself,
struggling to break free of your bulging edges,
straining toward that glistening other
just beyond you,
yet in your path?

Do you thrill with anticipated joy
in that last, speeded-up instant?
At the transformation,
are you awed by the increased power,
the speed,
of the two of you joined,
engulfing still others
in your mad rush down the pane?

Or do you dread the moment—
the collision—
the absorption—
the blending into one that erases both
and sends you
hurtling out of control
into that great,
anonymous
pool on the sill?

Archetypal

Tassajara, 59 Degrees

The native Californians
are surprised at my clothing—
the sweatshirts, wool socks,
even on this mild day.

"Aren't you from Minnesota?"
I am,
and I don't know
how to tell them
what so much ice
teaches.

Audioguide: Pompeii

Five Euro—a small price
for such a detailed account
of suffering,
and you can listen
in comfort as you walk,
if you don't mind ash on your feet,
and,
at your back,
the hot breath of the dead.

Poetry Workshop at a Buddhist Monastery

We are all so mindful here
of our steps
our voices
the way we cast our eyes
except for you
who come in late
loud
with big gestures
to sit
in your bikini top
knocking the altar with your backpack
theatrically swatting and killing flies
while we read poems aloud
in reverent tones.

How deftly you hold the mirror.

The Lady of Shalott

could not weave the world
and live in it,
just as I can not write a thing
that is here.
It is only in absence
that the reflection comes,
the warp and weft under my hands
showing me for the first time
what it is
I have seen.

In the Egyptian Book of the Dead

The dead eat their way
back to heaven,
swallowing again the gods
they have lost,
until only the heart
remains human;
only the heart
is judged.

Weighed against one feather,
will my freighted heart tip low,
or balance,
each chamber scrubbed thin,
a weightless parchment of loss?

In Absentia

Achilles absent was Achilles still . . .
                              The Iliad, 22.41

Hole, space,
gap—
none of these.

Daily weight,
stone in my chest,
nine years dragging
a plow through mud.

Airless.

Archetypal

In Florence I saw him, expecting perfection,
but marble expression of Beautiful Male
had eyes that were lifeless,
no music behind them,
no love for Bathsheba,
no echoes of Psalms.

I saw her in Paris
and wept for her losses;
mother of Cupid, destroyer of Troy
had arms that were missing,
and what good is beauty,
no dove wing to fondle,
no warrior to hold?

I reach for you finally,
you see me completely,
mingling breath
into flesh
into stone.

You Must Change Your Life

You may have to leave
your head behind,
give up the clinging arms,
the legs
with which you run.

All that will be left

your heart
your breath

will be everything
you need.

Notes:

"Transom": An alternate definition for the word *transom*: "The horizontal beam on a cross or gallows."

"Dear Immovable Object": Quotes are from the *Tao Te Ching*, with the exception of the first one, which is from Homer's *Odyssey*.

"Matriarchy": This poem is a response to e.e. cummings' poem "the Cambridge ladies who live in furnished souls."

"In Absentia": The initial quote is from Pope's translation of *The Iliad*. The poem also obliquely references *The Iliad*, 22.41, when the dead Achilles says to Odysseus, "By god, I'd rather slave on earth for another man—some dirt-poor tenant farmer who scrapes to keep alive—than rule down here over all the breathless dead."

"You Must Change Your Life": See "Archaic Torso of Apollo" by Ranier Maria Rilke.

LouAnn Shepard Muhm is a poet and teacher from Park Rapids, Minnesota. Her poems have appeared in many journals including *Dust & Fire, The Talking Stick, Red River Review* and *CALYX*. She was a finalist for the Creekwalker Poetry Prize (2007) and the Late Blooms Postcard Series (2007). Muhm was a 2006 recipient of the Minnesota State Arts Board Artist Initiative Grant in Poetry. Her chapbook, *Dear Immovable,* was published in 2006 by Pudding House Press. *Breaking the Glass* is her first full-length poetry collection.